in the garden

explore & discover
the New Zealand
backyard

Ned Barraud & Gillian Candler

craig potton publishing

To my wife Niamh — NB
For my parents — GC

Ned Barraud is an illustrator with a keen passion for the natural world. When not illustrating, he works on films at Weta Digital as a texture artist. He lives in Wellington, with his wife, three children, one dog, one budgie and seven chickens, and spends much of his spare time mucking around in the veggie garden.

Gillian Candler has been a teacher and worked in educational publishing for many years. She now works as a writer and consultant. She enjoys seeing the creatures that live in and visit her wild garden in Pukerua Bay.

First published in 2013 by Craig Potton Publishing

Craig Potton Publishing
98 Vickerman Street, PO Box 555, Nelson,
New Zealand
www.craigpotton.co.nz

Illustrations © Ned Barraud; text © Gillian Candler

ISBN PB 978-1-877517-99-0; HB 978-1-927213-02-5

Printed in China by Midas Printing International Ltd

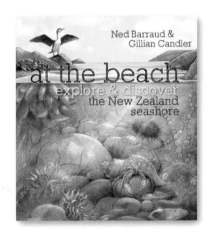

Also by Ned Barraud and Gillian Candler, *At the Beach: explore and discover the New Zealand seashore*, 2013 NZ Post Children's Book Awards finalist, winner of the 2013 LIANZA Elsie Locke Medal for non-fiction.

contents

There's a rustling and a buzzing in the garden.

Something chirps and sings. The garden is alive with animals and plants.
For the creatures that live here, the garden is a wild place. Insects, spiders, lizards
and other animals need clever ways to survive. Some live deep under the soil,
some hide during the daytime, some are camouflaged
so they can't be seen easily.

Birds visit the garden, eating insects,
nectar and fruit. Some stay and build
nests in the hedge or the trees.

The garden has many secrets. Look carefully, as you turn the pages of this book to discover the animals and plants that live in the garden.

5

It is spring. The garden has been dug. Seeds and young plants have just been planted. Sun and rain will help the plants to grow, but they also need food that the soil provides.

Bees and butterflies are visiting the garden. **Look at pages 18-21** to find out more about the bees, butterflies and moths that are in the pictures of this book.

Small animals are living in the soil,
the compost and the decaying log.

Look for signs of animals.
The snails leave shiny trails behind them.
The song thrush has eaten some of the snails and
left their empty shells on the ground.
Worm casts show where worms have
come up out of the soil.

The blackbird knows there are worms and grass grubs in the
lawn. It is listening and looking for them, hoping to catch
food to take back to the baby birds in its nest.

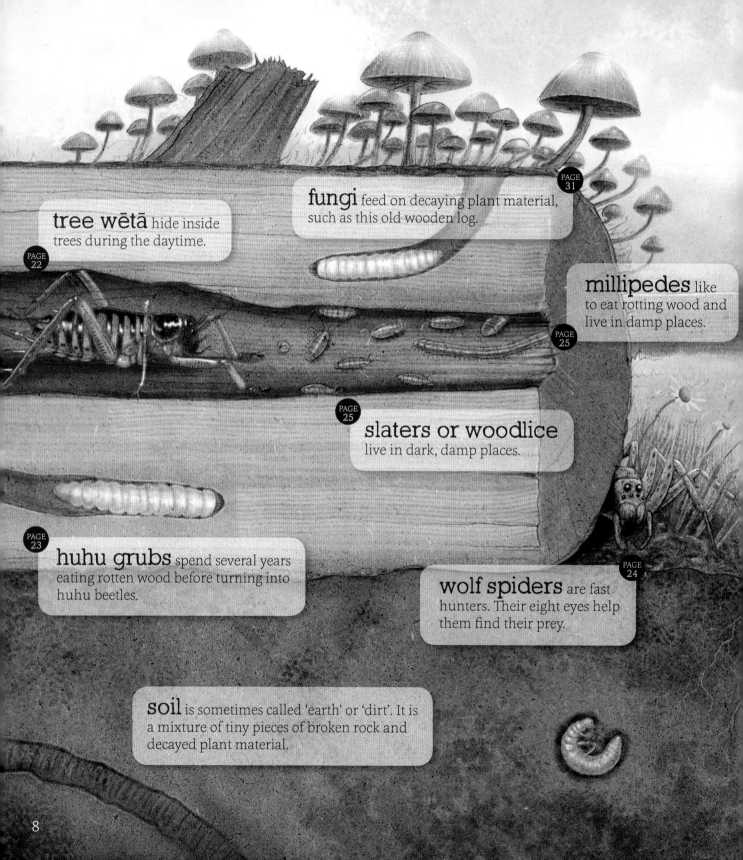

fungi feed on decaying plant material, such as this old wooden log.

PAGE 31

tree wētā hide inside trees during the daytime.

PAGE 22

millipedes like to eat rotting wood and live in damp places.

PAGE 25

PAGE 25

slaters or woodlice live in dark, damp places.

huhu grubs spend several years eating rotten wood before turning into huhu beetles.

PAGE 23

wolf spiders are fast hunters. Their eight eyes help them find their prey.

PAGE 24

soil is sometimes called 'earth' or 'dirt'. It is a mixture of tiny pieces of broken rock and decayed plant material.

What lives in the ground?

song thrushes eat snails, worms, insects and spiders.

PAGE 27

PAGE 26

blackbirds like to feed on the ground.

centipedes eat insects, worms and slugs.

PAGE 25

PAGE 23

This **grass grub** will grow into a **bronze beetle** if it can escape the blackbird's beak.

worms eat dead plants and soil, leaving worm casts (worm poo) behind them.

PAGE 25

9

In summer, the noisy male cicadas are calling for females. Plums are ripening on the tree and the flax has almost finished flowering.

Birds have come to the garden to find food. **Look at pages 26-27** to find out which birds are in the garden and what they are eating.

Plants make good places for animals to live. Some insects are hiding among the leaves and twigs, camouflaged so birds can't spot them.

It is easier to see the colourful butterflies, moths and caterpillars. Their bright colours warn birds that they are poisonous.

For a closer look at what lives on the plants, **turn to pages 12-13**. For what lives in the trees, **turn to pages 14-15**.

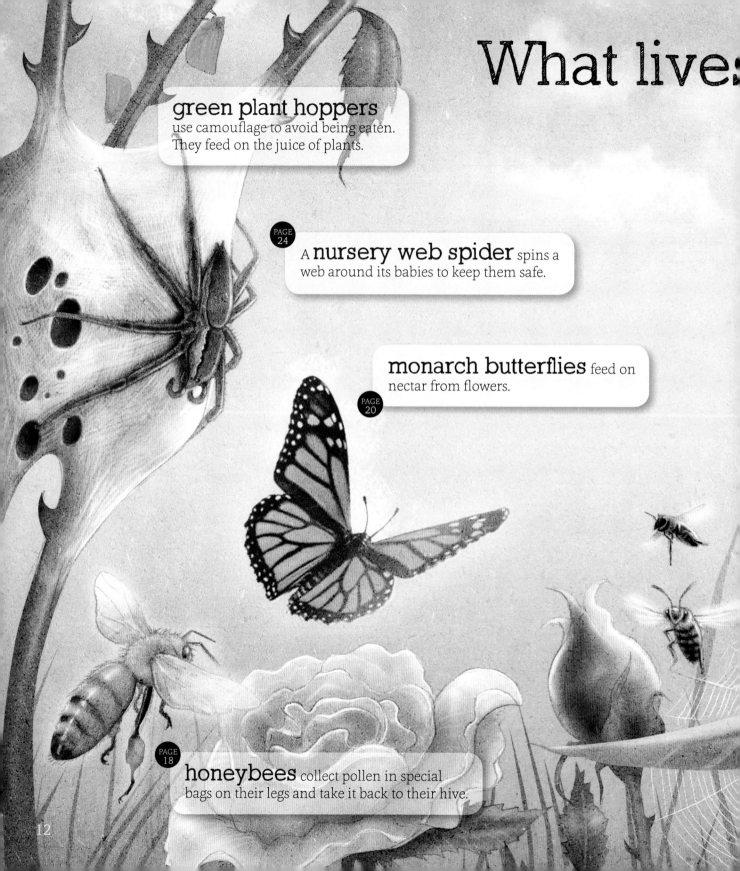

green plant hoppers use camouflage to avoid being eaten. They feed on the juice of plants.

PAGE 24 A **nursery web spider** spins a web around its babies to keep them safe.

monarch butterflies feed on nectar from flowers. PAGE 20

PAGE 18 **honeybees** collect pollen in special bags on their legs and take it back to their hive.

on the plants?

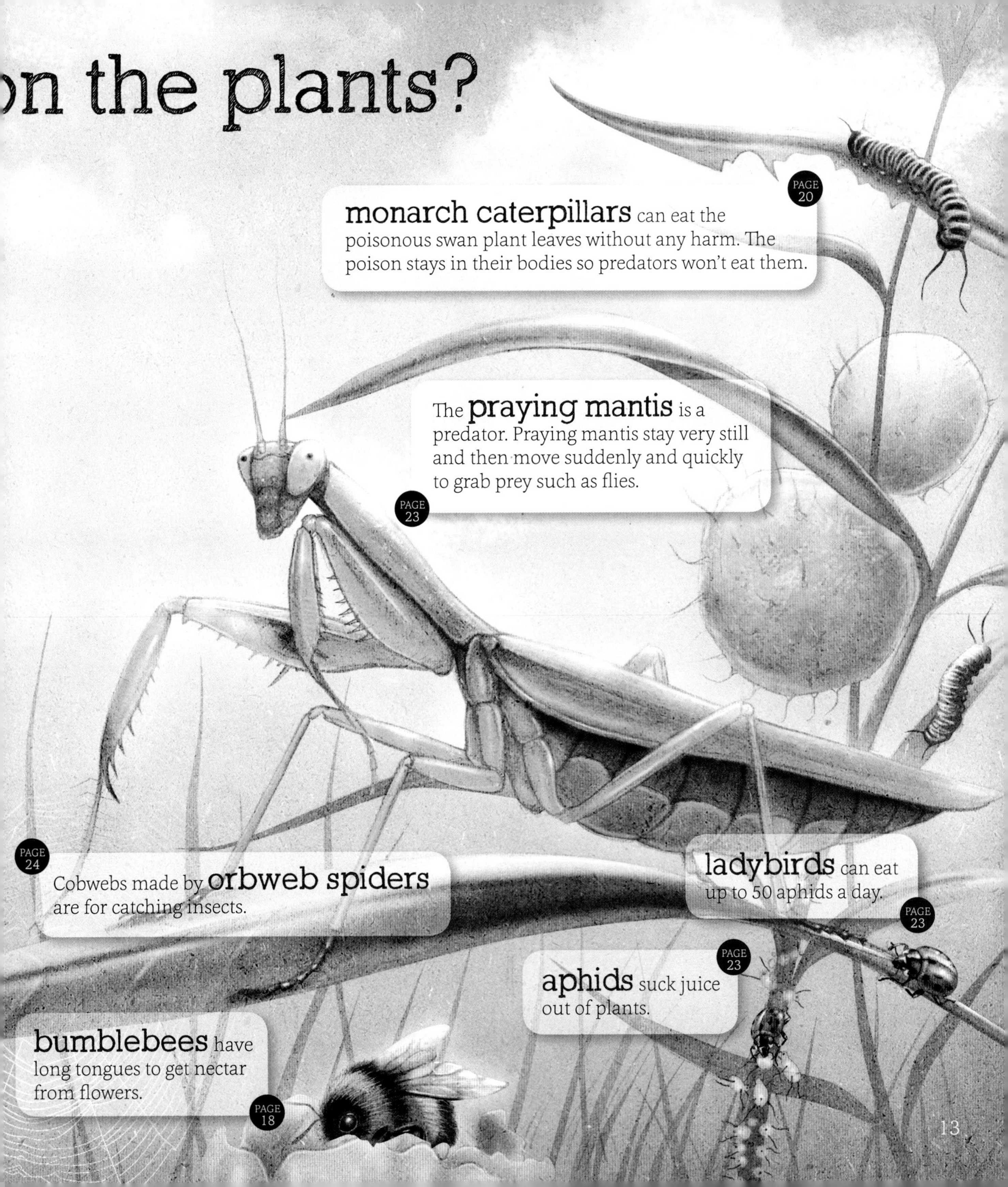

PAGE 20

monarch caterpillars can eat the poisonous swan plant leaves without any harm. The poison stays in their bodies so predators won't eat them.

The **praying mantis** is a predator. Praying mantis stay very still and then move suddenly and quickly to grab prey such as flies.

PAGE 23

PAGE 24

Cobwebs made by **orbweb spiders** are for catching insects.

ladybirds can eat up to 50 aphids a day.

PAGE 23

PAGE 23

aphids suck juice out of plants.

bumblebees have long tongues to get nectar from flowers.

PAGE 18

myna birds feed on insects, spiders, worms and fruit.
PAGE 26

wasps eat insects and fruit.
PAGE 18

cicadas leave behind their old skins when they grow.
PAGE 22

fantails catch insects in the air as they fly about.
PAGE 26

lichen is growing on the tree.
PAGE 31

What lives in the trees?

The **tui** has got pollen on its feathers. It helps the flax by moving pollen from one flower to another.

PAGE 27

silvereyes eat fruit as well as insects.

PAGE 26

stick insects are well camouflaged, they look like twigs.

PAGE 22

skinks like warm places. These rocks are hot from the sunshine.

PAGE 28

geckos are hard to see in the daytime, but you can sometimes find their old skins that they have left behind.

PAGE 28

In the dark of night, when most birds are asleep, other animals visit the garden.

A huhu beetle is flying clumsily, searching for a mate. Slugs and snails have come out of hiding to look for food, but the hedgehog has found them first.

A possum is visiting the garden too, looking for fruit and anything else tasty it can find.

The neighbour's cat is on the prowl. Maybe it will catch something tonight.

Geckos are hunting for insects and trying to stay out of the way of the other animals.

Look closely and you will see rats and mice that are searching for food too.

17

pollen bags

bumblebee

Bumblebees live in smaller groups than honeybees. They usually make their nest in holes in the ground or in trees. They are the only bee with a tongue long enough to get nectar from red clover, and this is why people brought them to New Zealand. 25 mm

bee and wasp facts

- Honeybees, bumblebees and common wasps are all *introduced* to New Zealand. There are native bees and wasps too, but they aren't brightly coloured and mostly live in native bush.
- Honeybees, bumblebees and drone flies help plants by taking pollen from one flower to the other. You can read more about this on pages 30-31.

sting

honeybee pi

Honeybees are social insects – they live together in large groups. Each beehive has one queen, some drones (male bees) and hundreds of worker bees. The worker bees collect nectar and pollen from flowers. They make wax to build their nest and for storing honey. Honeybees use dances to tell each other where to find flowers. 12 mm

common wasp wāpi

Watch out for wasps! They like sugary food and drinks, so make sure they aren't sharing yours. Wasps eat insects and spiders too. They don't collect pollen or make honey. They nest in warm places, such as sunny banks or even in house roofs. 20 mm

bees, wasps, flies & ants

drone fly

Looks like a bee? Look carefully and you can see that the orange stripes of a drone fly don't always join across its back. Drone flies don't sting but they do eat nectar and pollen. 13 mm

ant pōpokorua

Ants live in colonies, and each ant has a different role in the colony. There is usually only one queen ant, but there are many soldiers, nurses, and workers. Ants are very strong. They can carry up to 50 times their own weight. They are scavengers and will eat dead insects as well as sugary foods. Up to 10 mm

stinging facts

- Bumblebees and honeybees will usually only sting if you stand on them or provoke them.
- Honeybees leave their stinger behind, so they die when they sting.
- Wasps can sting more than once and are more aggressive than bees.

Warning: For some people stings cause an allergic reaction. Get help from an adult straightaway if you are stung by a bee or wasp.

house fly rango

Flies have a good sense of smell, which helps them find food and places to lay their eggs. They do this on rotting food or plants so that the young maggots will have food to eat when they hatch. 8 mm

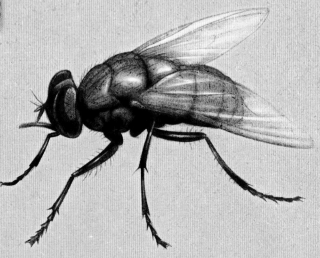

butterflies & moths

pūrerehua

from egg to butterfly

Eggs Butterflies and moths lay their eggs on plants that the caterpillar can eat.

Caterpillar anuhe Caterpillars (also called larvae) hatch out of the eggs. They eat and eat until they are ready to form a chrysalis.

Chrysalis tūngoungou The caterpillar stops eating and becomes a chrysalis. Inside the chrysalis it changes into a butterfly or moth.

Butterfly The butterfly emerges from the chrysalis and flys off to find a mate. The female lays eggs and the cycle starts again.

butterfly and moths: what's the difference?

- Butterflies and moths aren't really that different. They belong to the same large group of insects and they both feed on nectar.
- Most butterflies are active during the day and most moths fly around at night. But there are some moths that fly during the day.
- One way you can tell the difference is to look closely at the antennae. Butterflies have knobs or clubs on the end of their antennae and moths do not.

monarch butterfly kahuku

Monarch butterflies lay their eggs on swan plants or other plants in the milkweed family.
Wingspan up to 100 mm

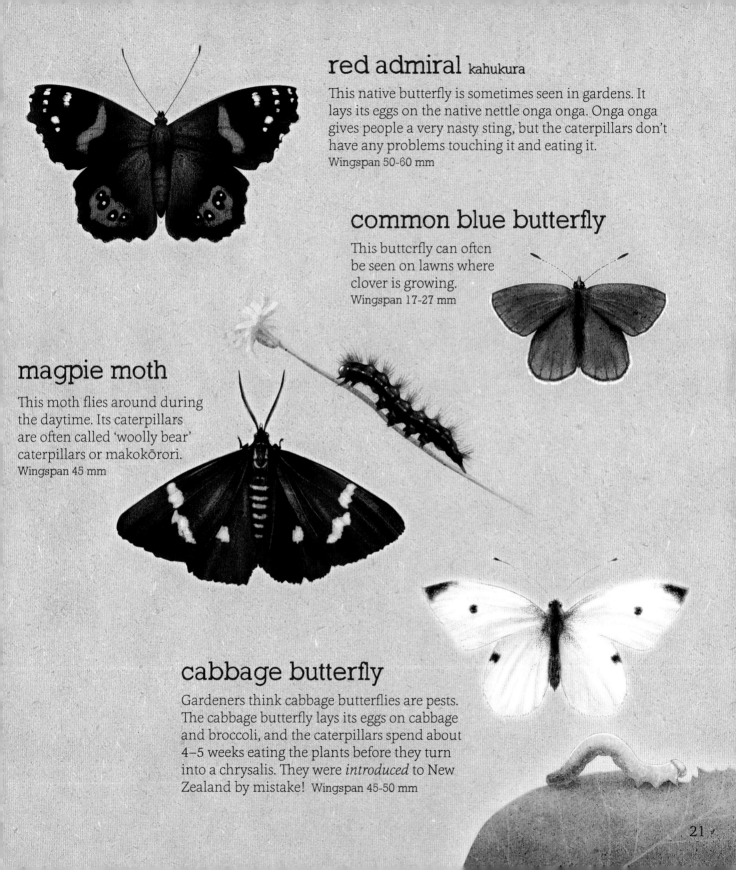

red admiral kahukura

This native butterfly is sometimes seen in gardens. It lays its eggs on the native nettle onga onga. Onga onga gives people a very nasty sting, but the caterpillars don't have any problems touching it and eating it.
Wingspan 50-60 mm

common blue butterfly

This butterfly can often be seen on lawns where clover is growing.
Wingspan 17-27 mm

magpie moth

This moth flies around during the daytime. Its caterpillars are often called 'woolly bear' caterpillars or makokōrori.
Wingspan 45 mm

cabbage butterfly

Gardeners think cabbage butterflies are pests. The cabbage butterfly lays its eggs on cabbage and broccoli, and the caterpillars spend about 4–5 weeks eating the plants before they turn into a chrysalis. They were *introduced* to New Zealand by mistake! Wingspan 45-50 mm

more insects

cicada kihikihi

The young of cicadas spend years living underground, eating roots of plants. In summer, if they are old enough, they come out of the ground and climb up trees or poles. Then they climb out of their old skin and fly away. The males vibrate their body to make the noise that cicadas are famous for. This is to attract female cicadas.
Up to 40 mm including wings

insect facts

- All the animals on pages 18-23 are insects. They all have six legs and two antennae. Some insects have wings and can fly.
- There are about 20,000 species of insects in New Zealand.

Stick insect rō

Stick insects can be green or brown, smooth or rough. They feed on leaves at night. During the day they stay quite still so birds can't see them.
Up to 200 mm including its front legs.

wētā

Weta only live in New Zealand. They fight and will lift up their spiky legs if they feel threatened. The spike on the back end of this female tree weta is an ovipositor, which helps it to lay eggs. 40 mm

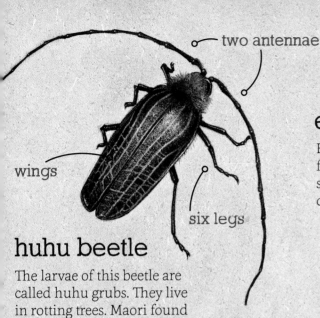

two antennae

wings

six legs

huhu beetle

The larvae of this beetle are called huhu grubs. They live in rotting trees. Maori found them to be good to eat. 40-50 mm

earwig hiore kakati

Earwigs eat plants, fruit and other insects. They use their pincers for grabbing and holding insect prey. There are lots of different stories about how earwigs got their strange English name – but don't worry, they aren't interested in your ears! 10-20 mm

aphid

Aphids suck juice from plants. They breed quickly and there can be quite large numbers on a plant. They are a favourite food of birds, praying mantis and ladybirds. Up to 2-4 mm

ladybird mumutawa

Ladybirds can be red, yellow or orange. Both the ladybird and its larvae eat aphids. Ladybirds are beetles and can fly. Up to 5 mm

bronze beetle tutaeruru

Bronze beetles are the adult form of grass grubs. They feed on leaves and fruit.

pest or helper?

- Aphids and other creatures that eat plants are often called pests.

- Some gardeners use poisons to get rid of pests. This can also harm the 'good' animals that eat these pests, such as ladybirds. Gardeners need to know 'who eats who' and think carefully before they use poisons.

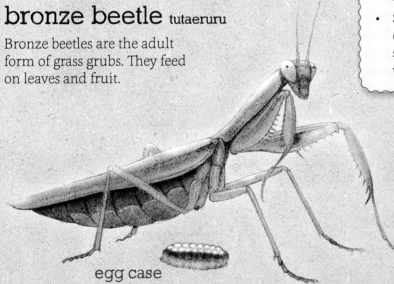

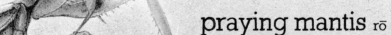
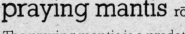

egg case

praying mantis rō

The praying mantis is a predator. It uses its camouflage to pretend to be a leaf, then it jumps suddenly onto its prey. It eats flies, aphids and other insects. You might find its egg case on a fence or branch.

30-40 mm including its wings

spiders, snails worms & more

orbweb spider

This orbweb spider makes a sticky web to catch insects. You might wonder why it doesn't get stuck in its own web. It covers its legs with an oily liquid so it can't get caught. Once the orbweb spider has caught an insect, it wraps it up to eat later. 12 mm

wolf spider

Wolf spiders don't build webs to live in or to catch prey; instead they go hunting. Female wolf spiders carry their eggs around with them, and when the baby spiders hatch they carry them around too. 7 mm

nursery web spider

The female nursery web spider makes a web to protect its babies. About 200 baby spiders are kept safe in the web until they are big enough to leave.
18 mm

spider facts

- The Maori name for spider is pūngāwerewere.
- All spiders have eight legs.
- All spiders are carnivorous. Some kinds of spiders are hunters, like the wolf spider, but others wait for their prey to become trapped in a web or tunnel.
- Be careful! Some spiders will bite if you disturb them.
- Spiders are eaten by wasps and birds.

worm facts

- Worms are great for the soil. They mix it up and make tunnels to let air in as well as eating decaying plant material.
- Worm casts (worm poo) are full of nutrients that are good for the soil.
- Garden worms like living in soil and compost.
- There are many kinds of native worms that live in the bush, some of which grow over a metre long.
- People say that worms will grow into two worms if they are cut in half but this is not true.

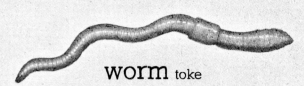

worm toke

Worms don't have bones. Their body segments have muscles that help them move. If you see a bump around its middle, this is where the worm is storing its eggs.

eyes on stalks

snail

Snails are slow movers, taking about a minute to cover just 10 cm of pathway.

Shell diameter up to 32 mm

slater

These strange-looking creatures, also called woodlice, are related to crabs and prawns. They eat dead plant material so do a good job of cleaning up in the garden. They can only live where it is wet or damp. Up to 17 mm

centipede or millipede? weri

Centipedes are carnivorous – they eat insects, worms and slugs. Millipedes are vegetarian – they eat plant material. Both have lots of legs, although not as many as their names suggest. If you look closely, you can see that centipedes have one pair of legs under each segment and millipedes have two. Up to 100 mm

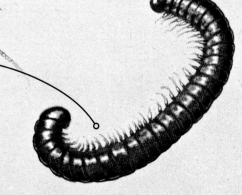

25

birds

fantail
pīwakawaka

Fantails are insect eaters. Their tail helps them make quick movements in the air as they hunt flying insects. Fantails build several nests and lay more than one lot of eggs each year. 160 mm

male

blackbird
manu pango

female

The female blackbird isn't black! Her brown colour makes it easier to hide in hedges and among the grass. Both parents feed the baby blackbirds. Sometimes you can see the young birds hopping along behind their parents waiting for food. 250 mm

silvereye
tauhou

Silvereyes are also called waxeyes or white-eyes. Their Maori name means 'stranger' as they arrived in New Zealand nearly 200 years ago, having flown 2000 km from Australia. 120 mm

myna birds
maina

Myna (or mynah) birds only live in the middle and north of the North Island. They are bossy and will attack other birds. They eat just about anything, including the eggs and chicks of other birds. 240 mm

chaffinch
pahirini

26

Chaffinches are members of the finch family. Other finches that are sometimes seen in gardens are greenfinches and goldfinches. Finches use their powerful beaks and gizzards for grinding up seeds. 150 mm

starling
tāringi

Starlings eat insects, snails and spiders as well as fruit and nectar from plants. They nest in holes in trees or buildings. 210 mm

bird facts

- The birds on these pages are the most common birds in New Zealand gardens, according to the Garden Bird Survey held every year.
- Birds don't have teeth. The food they eat goes into their stomach and then into a gizzard, where it is ground up.
- Some birds, such as silvereyes, feed together in flocks. This means they can warn each other of danger and also help each other find food.
- Blackbirds and song thrushes prefer to feed on their own and will try to defend their territory from other birds.

song thrush

Song thrushes can be seen hopping around in the garden. Their favourite food is snails. 230 mm

Tui eat nectar from flowering plants, such as flax. They also eat insects and fruit. Tui are able to imitate noises, such as car alarms or phones, as well as the songs of other birds. 300 mm

tui tūī

female

male

sparrow
tiu

Sparrows are the most common garden birds in New Zealand. They were introduced to New Zealand because people thought they would help farmers by eating insect pests, but they eat more seeds than insects. Now many people think sparrows are pests. 140 mm

27

lizards & mammals

lizard facts
mokomoko

- Lizards like sunny rock walls and other places where they can keep warm and hide.
- Geckos and skinks are lizards that are native to New Zealand.
- One way you can tell them apart is that geckos have an obvious neck and bulging eyes; skinks have a narrow head and neck.
- Both geckos and skinks can drop off their tail if it is grabbed by a predator. A new tail will grow in its place.
- Many of New Zealand's geckos and skinks are rare. Because of the threat that they might become extinct, all of our geckos and skinks are protected by law.

gecko
mokomoko

Geckos are great climbers and can even walk upside down. They mostly go hunting for food at night. In the daytime you might surprise one hiding in a warm place. Geckos can be green or brown. Up to 180 mm including tail

skink
mokomoko

Skinks are more easily seen than geckos because they hunt insects in the daytime. They have smooth skins, unlike geckos, which have baggy skins. Up to 130 mm including tail

rat kiore

There are three different kinds of rat in New Zealand: the native kiore, the Norway rat and the ship rat. If you see rats in your garden, they are most likely ship rats. They are good climbers and will try to nest in house roofs. Up to 460 mm including tail

mouse kiore

Mice can get through very small gaps, which means that they will often find a way to get into people's houses. They eat seeds and berries as well as insects and worms. Up to 200 mm including tail

mammal facts

- Mammals give birth to live young and their mothers feed them with milk from their teats.
- All the mammals on these pages were introduced to New Zealand and are a major threat to New Zealand's native animals – birds, insects and lizards.
- New Zealand's only native mammals are bats and these are quite rare, even in forests.

cat ngeru

Many people have cats as pets and let their cats out to wander around. So even if you don't have a cat, other people's cats might visit your garden.

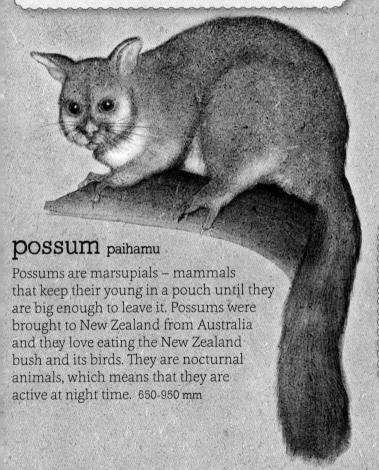

possum paihamu

Possums are marsupials – mammals that keep their young in a pouch until they are big enough to leave it. Possums were brought to New Zealand from Australia and they love eating the New Zealand bush and its birds. They are nocturnal animals, which means that they are active at night time. 650-950 mm

pet or pest?

Pests are animals or plants that are a nuisance or can do damage. Some people like to have cats, rats and even mice as pets. But for native animals they are all pests. If you have a cat, you can help make your pet less of a pest by keeping it inside at night and putting a bell around its neck.

hedgehog tuatete

Hedgehogs use their prickles as a defence. They roll up into a ball of prickles if they feel threatened. You might hear them snuffling in your garden at night, but you can also see them during the day. In cold areas they hibernate, or sleep all through winter. This is how they can survive cold weather. 300-380 mm

plants & fungi

plant facts

- Grasses, vegetables, herbs, trees, ferns and weeds are all plants.
- All plants need air, water and light to grow.
- Many plants have flowers, including grasses and some trees.
- Insects such as bees and butterflies visit flowers and pollinate them, helping the plant to make seeds.

flower

The **anther** has pollen on it, which brushes off onto the insect.

petal Its colour or smell attracts insects to the nectar.

The **stigma** is waiting for pollen to be brushed on to it. The pollen then travels down to the ovary.

ovary Here is the part of the flower where the seeds form.

nectar attracts insects butterflies and moths to the flower.

The **plant** grows up towards the light.

leaf A green substance in leaves, called chlorophyll, helps the plant turn sunlight into food for the plant.

life-cycle
of the
pea plant

flower
When the plant is big enough, it grows flowers. These open up and insects visit to pollinate them.

The **stem** holds the plant up to the light. Food travels inside the stem between the roots and the leaves.

seeds Once the flower dies, seeds develop inside a pod.

roots hold the plant in the ground, and take in water and food from the soil.

When the **seed** is planted and watered, it grows roots and becomes a young plant.

People pick pea pods and eat the peas inside them, before they have dried out and become seeds that can grow.

what is a weed?

Weeds are plants that are growing where they are not wanted. Sometimes they are just a plant people don't like, such as black nightshade or dandelions. But weeds may also be harmful to other plants, smothering them and preventing them from growing.

trees are plants with woody stems. The woody stem or trunk needs to be strong enough to hold the tree up. If you cut through a tree trunk, you can see its growth rings. Each ring is roughly a year of growth.

black nightshade   dandelion

fungus, fungi

Fungi are different from plants. They don't have leaves and can't make their own food.

Instead, fungi get their food from compost, rotting wood or decaying plants. Fungi grow in damp places and don't need light to grow. The part of the fungus that you can see is actually its fruit. Most of the fungus is underground. Fungi can be many different colours and shapes.

rimu tree

A **lichen** is a combination of a fungus and an alga. It doesn't have roots so it can grow on tree, rocks and buildings.

fly agaric fungi

basket fungi

31

glossary

camouflage Colour or shape of an animal that matches its surroundings so that the animal is hard to see.

carnivore An animal that eats other animals

compost Decayed plant material that has broken down until it almost looks like soil.

decay When living things such as plants die, the leaves, stems, roots, flowers and wood start to rot and break down; this is called decay.

flock A group of animals, such as birds.

gizzard A special stomach that is able to grind food. Some birds swallow stones, which stay in their gizzard and help with the grinding.

introduced Animals or plants that are not native to New Zealand.

larva A young insect at an earlier stage of development, that looks quite different from an adult e.g. caterpillar.

native Animals or plants that have lived in New Zealand for thousands of years

nocturnal An animal that is active at nighttime.

plant material Any part of a plant, such as, leaves, stems, roots, flowers or wood.

predator An animal that hunts and eats other animals.

scavenger An animal that eats anything it can find, including animals that are already dead.

threatened species A species of animal that might die out (become extinct).

index

find out more

Visit your local botanic garden, check out books from your local library or go to these websites:

Information about insects and other garden creatures:

www.landcareresearch.co.nz Bug identification and Garden bird survey

www.kcc.org.nz Kiwi conservation club

www.teara.govt.nz Te Ara–The Encyclopaedia of New Zealand

www.monarch.org.nz The Monarch Butterfly New Zealand Trust

www.reptiles.org.nz The New Zealand Herpetological Society

http://www.doc.govt.nz/getting-involved/home-and-garden/ ideas for garden projects, such as weta motels, tracking tunnels, bird feeders

Information for parents & teachers about this book: *www.craigpotton.co.nz/in-the-garden*